To our little Marcello,
born along with *A Boy Named Giotto*

Copyright © 1998 by Edizioni Arka, Milano
Translation copyright © 1999 by Jonathan Galassi
All rights reserved
Originally published in Italy under the title
Un bambino di nome Giotto by Edizioni Arka, 1998
Distributed in Canada by Douglas & McIntyre Ltd.
Printed in Italy by Grafiche Seven S.p.A.
Bound in Italy by Zanardi Editoriale S.p.A.
First American edition, 1999
3 5 7 9 11 10 8 6 4 2

Library of Congress Cataloging-in-Publication Data
Guarnieri, Paolo.
  [Bambino di nome Giotto. English]
  A boy named Giotto / Paolo Guarnieri ; pictures by Bimba Landmann ;
translated by Jonathan Galassi. — 1st American ed.
      p.   cm.
  Summary: Eight-year-old Giotto the shepherd boy confesses his dream of becoming
an artist to the painter Cimabue, who teaches him how to make marvelous pigments
from minerals, flowers, and eggs and takes him on as his pupil.
  ISBN 0-374-30931-0
  1. Giotto, 1266?–1337—Juvenile fiction. [1. Giotto, 1266?–1337—Fiction.
2. Cimabue—Fiction. 3. Artists—Fiction. 4. Shepherds—Fiction. 5. Italy—Fiction.]
I. Landmann, Bimba, ill. II. Galassi, Jonathan. III. Title.
PZ7.G93415Bo 1999
[E]—dc21   98-42047

A BOY NAMED
Giotto

Paolo Guarnieri · Pictures by Bimba Landmann

TRANSLATED BY JONATHAN GALASSI

FARRAR STRAUS GIROUX   NEW YORK

Every morning, little Giotto leads his father's flock to the pasture. He ambles distractedly, thinking of a wish he would like to make come true. A wish that, for now, he can't tell anyone.

In the pasture, instead of keeping watch over the flock, Giotto spends his time sketching.

He draws pictures of sheep, trees, and birds on everything he finds: on light-colored stones with a piece of charcoal, on dark stones with a piece of chalk, in the sand with a stick.

They are so beautiful that passersby often stop to admire them.

"Too bad a gust of wind or a rain shower is all it takes to erase them," says the shepherd boy, sighing.

He draws till he hears the evening bells tolling in the distance. Then he hurries to gather the sheep and take them back to their pen.

Master Bondone, his father, waits for him to come home every evening. He doesn't trust Giotto. "Always with his head in the clouds!" he says of his boy as he counts the sheep.

This evening, in fact, he's angry. "One's missing! It would have to be tonight, when I can't go find it," he scolds. "There's a great feast in town. But you're not coming. You're staying home!"

Giotto is sad, not because of his punishment, but because he's lost a lamb. How will it survive the night, he worries.

He would love to draw it on the bare wall of his room with a piece of chalk, but his father would only get angry again. "All you do is scribble," he'd say, as he has done so many times.

Suddenly Giotto hears voices and footsteps in the street.

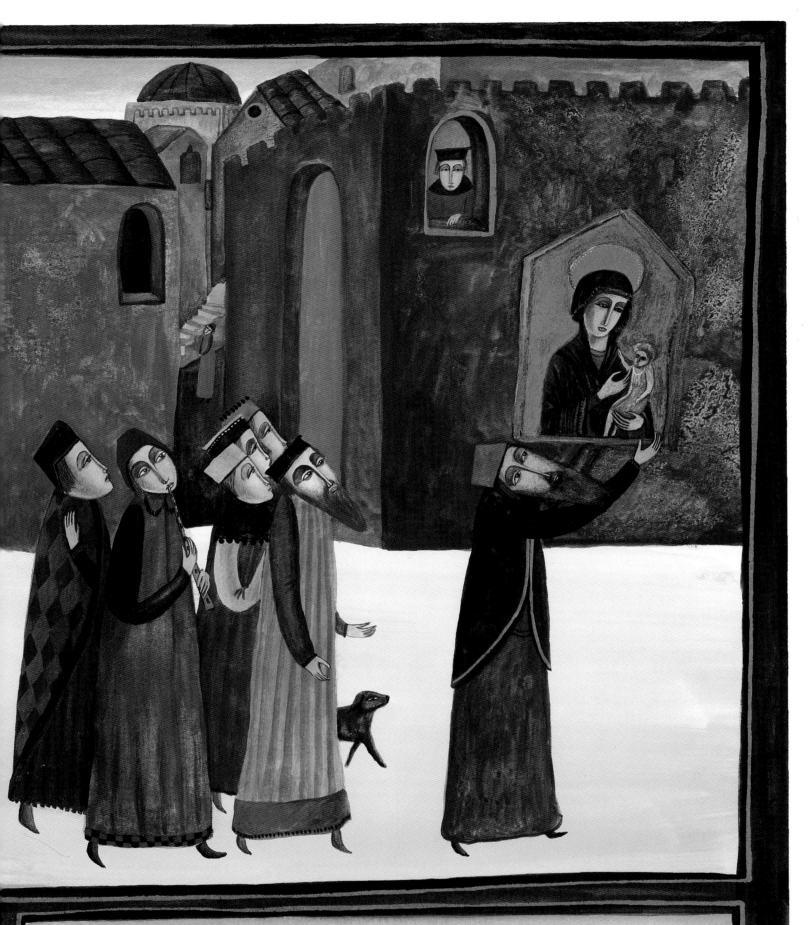

Curious, Giotto looks out. He sees his father in the procession. He's about to pull back inside, when he stops, as if enchanted: the setting sun is reflected in the gold of a beautiful painting being carried through the streets.

"Who made it? And how?" he asks in amazement.

So strong is his curiosity, and his wonder, that Giotto disobeys his father. He leaves the house, slips in among the crowd, and enters the great church along with them.

"The painter of the *Madonna with Child* is called Cimabue," he hears someone say.

Giotto would like to ask him where he found the colors to paint his picture, and to confide in him that he, too, would like to be a painter when he grows up.

"Certainly a painter would understand me," he thinks. But he doesn't dare approach Cimabue.

Yet he dares to follow him as he's leaving . . .

. . . and from a window he peers into the artist's workshop.

"Signor Cimabue!" he calls.

The painter turns.

"Come in, don't be afraid," he tells the boy.

Giotto isn't afraid. "I'm only a shepherd, but I'd like . . ."

The painter listens. He listens as the boy tells him his greatest wish.

And then he tells him a secret, too.

"To paint the way you want, you need colored powders. They're called pigments, and they come from minerals and flowers."

Now it's Giotto's turn to listen. He does so with such fascination that the painter hands him some red powder.

"Grind this in a mortar with a few drops of water," he tells him. "Next, take these eggs and beat the yolks thoroughly in another mortar. Now mix them with the colored paste."

Then, on a wood panel covered with gesso, the painter draws a figure and helps the boy apply the paint.

"Neither rain nor wind will ever erase this picture," thinks the shepherd.

It doesn't seem real when the painter gives him some of his colored powders, and promises, "Tomorrow I'll come see your drawings on the stones."

What does seem real to Giotto is the dream he dreams that night. With his paints he gives life to the old stones of houses and palaces.

He makes pictures on broad walls, and everyone exclaims, "What a marvelous painter this boy is! Look! His figures seem alive!"

It's such a long, intense dream that in the morning his father
has to come and wake him.

"Up, get up!" he says, shaking him. "It's time to take the flock
to the pasture and find the lamb you lost."

Giotto starts walking. He carries a sack on his back, with some
of the colored powders inside.

All day he paints on rocks and stones.

He paints with such concentration that he forgets to look
for the lost lamb, he forgets to watch over the flock, he doesn't
hear the bells in the distance ringing the hours.

It starts to get dark. Giotto, as if rousing himself from a
waking dream, realizes he's late.

"Tonight Father will be angry again," he thinks.

He's about to collect the sheep when he hears footsteps on
the path and his father's voice calling him.

Giotto is afraid of being scolded, and hides. But then he hears more steps, another voice, greetings, and his father exclaims, "It's incredible! Here's the lamb my boy lost yesterday. And it seems to recognize its mother in your painting on this rock!"

"I'm afraid it's not mine," Cimabue corrects him. "No painter I know has ever succeeded in making a creature look so alive," he marvels. "But I recognize the paints I gave to a shepherd boy yesterday. If he's your son, I'd like to speak to you about him."

The painter and Master Bondone talk for a long time about young Giotto. And they continue their discussion that evening, at Master Bondone's home.

"Your son's drawings are anything but scribbles," Cimabue tells Giotto's parents. "I beg you, let him come study in my workshop in Florence."

"But he's still so young . . ." his mother says anxiously.

"And I need him to watch the sheep," his father adds.

"And I say I will make him into a great painter," Cimabue tells them with conviction.

"All right!" Master Bondone agrees at last. "But his mother has a point. He's only eight. I'll send him to you when he's a little older."

Seven years pass, and Giotto's father keeps his promise. And so, one morning, Giotto leaves his life as a shepherd boy behind.

In the workshop in Florence, he quickly learns the secrets of his calling, surpassing all his fellow students in skill.

Even though he's younger, I'll choose him as my assistant for my new fresco, Cimabue decides one day.

It's not easy to paint a fresco, and the two have to work with great speed. They need to cover the wall with a mixture of lime and very fine sand, then draw the figures and apply the paint before the mixture dries.

Nothing can be erased or retouched, but Giotto works with such a sure hand that Cimabue, amazed, lets him finish the picture by himself.

"The pupil has outdone the master," he thinks.

And he's not surprised when it's his youngest pupil who is called upon to paint the frescoes in the great church dedicated to Saint Francis, the poor friar who could talk with the wolves and the birds . . .

Giotto sets out for Assisi. He carries a sack on his shoulder, containing a great many colored powders.

The moment has come for him to paint frescoes that not even time will erase.